INDIANA
Macmillan/McGraw-Hill TIMELINKS

People and Places

PROGRAM AUTHORS
James A. Banks
Kevin P. Colleary
Linda Greenow
Walter C. Parker
Emily M. Schell
Dinah Zike

CONTRIBUTORS
Raymond C. Jones
Irma M. Olmedo

Macmillan/McGraw-Hill

Citizenship

PROGRAM AUTHORS

James A. Banks, Ph.D.
Kerry and Linda Killinger Professor
   of Diversity Studies and Director, Center
   for Multicultural Education
University of Washington
Seattle, Washington

Kevin P. Colleary, Ed.D.
Curriculum and Teaching Department
Graduate School of Education
Fordham University
New York, New York

Linda Greenow, Ph.D.
Associate Professor and Chair
Department of Geography
State University of New York at New Paltz
New Paltz, New York

Walter C. Parker, Ph.D.
Professor of Social Studies Education,
   Adjunct Professor of Political Science
University of Washington
Seattle, Washington

Emily M. Schell, Ed.D.
Visiting Professor, Teacher Education
San Diego State University
San Diego, California

Dinah Zike
Educational Consultant
Dinah-Mite Activities, Inc.
San Antonio, Texas

CONTRIBUTORS

Raymond C. Jones, Ph.D.
Director of Secondary Social Studies
   Education
Wake Forest University
Winston-Salem, North Carolina

Irma M. Olmedo
Associate Professor
University of Illinois-Chicago
College of Education
Chicago, Illinois

GRADE LEVEL REVIEWERS

Brigid Kemper
Second Grade Teacher
Brook Park Elementary School
Indianapolis, Indiana

Kathleen Clark
Second Grade Teacher
Edison Elementary School
Fraser, Michigan

Patricia Hinchliff
Second Grade Teacher
West Woods School
Hamden, Connecticut

Pamela South
Second Grade Teacher
Greenwood Elementary School
Princess Anne, Maryland

Karen Starr
Second Grade Teacher
Arthur Froberg Elementary School
Rockford, Illinois

EDITORIAL ADVISORY BOARD

Bradley R. Bakle
Assistant Superintendent
East Allen County Schools
New Haven, Indiana

Marilyn Barr
Assistant Superintendent for Instruction
Clyde-Savannah Central School
Clyde, New York

Lisa Bogle
Elementary Coordinator, K-5
Rutherford County Schools
Murfreesboro, Tennessee

Janice Buselt
Campus Support, Primary and ESOL
Wichita Public Schools
Wichita, Kansas

Kathy Cassioppi
Social Studies Coordinator
Rockford Public Schools, District 205
Rockford, Illinois

Denise Johnson, Ph.D.
Social Studies Supervisor
Knox County Schools
Knoxville, Tennessee

Steven Klein, Ph.D.
Social Studies Coordinator
Illinois School District U-46
Elgin, Illinois

Sondra Markman
Curriculum Director
Warren Township Board of Education
Warren Township, New Jersey

Cathy Nelson
Social Studies Coordinator
Columbus Public Schools
Columbus, Ohio

Holly Pies
Social Studies Coordinator
Vigo County Schools
Terre Haute, Indiana

Avon Ruffin
Social Studies County Supervisor
Winston-Salem/Forsyth Schools
Lewisville, North Carolina

Chuck Schierloh
Social Studies Curriculum Team Leader
Lima City Schools
Lima, Ohio

Bob Shamy
Social Studies Supervisor
East Brunswick Public Schools
East Brunswick, New Jersey

Judy Trujillo
Social Studies Coordinator
Columbia Missouri School District
Columbia, Missouri

Gayle Voyles
Director of the Center for Economic
   Education
Kansas City School District
Kansas City, Missouri

Todd Wigginton
Coordinator of Social Studies K-12
Metropolitan Nashville Public Schools
Nashville, Tennessee

RFB&D (V)
learning through listening

Students with print disabilities may be eligible to obtain an accessible, audio version of the pupil edition of this textbook. Please call Recording for the Blind & Dyslexic at 1-800-221-4792 for complete information.

The McGraw·Hill Companies

Macmillan McGraw-Hill

MHID 0-02-153378-4   ISBN 978-0-02-153378-7   Printed in the United States of America

3 4 5 6 7 8 9 10 058/043 13 12 11 10 09

People and Places

Table of Contents

Skills and Features

Maps

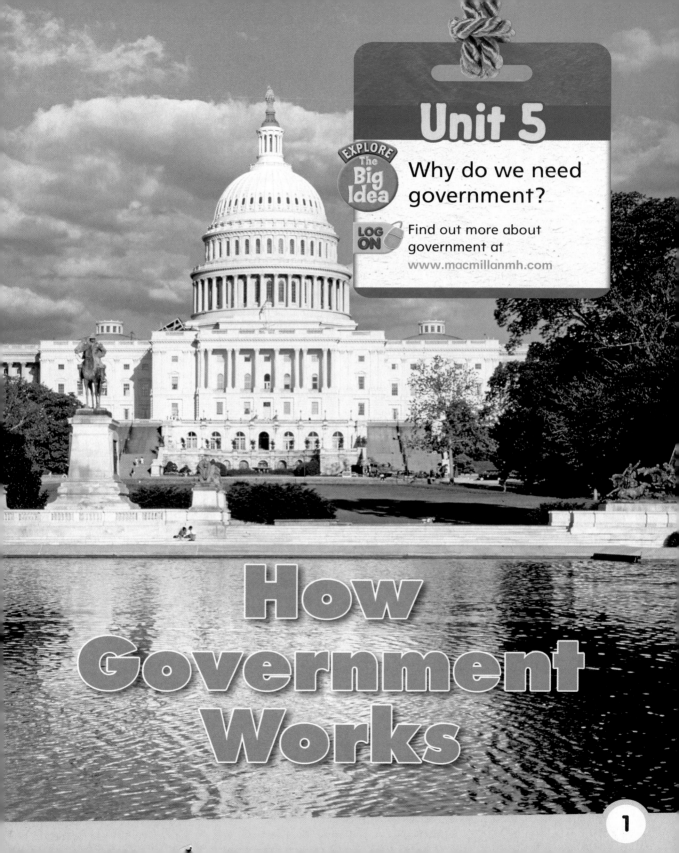

Unit 5

EXPLORE The Big Idea

Why do we need government?

LOG ON Find out more about government at www.macmillanmh.com

How Government Works

People, Places, and Events

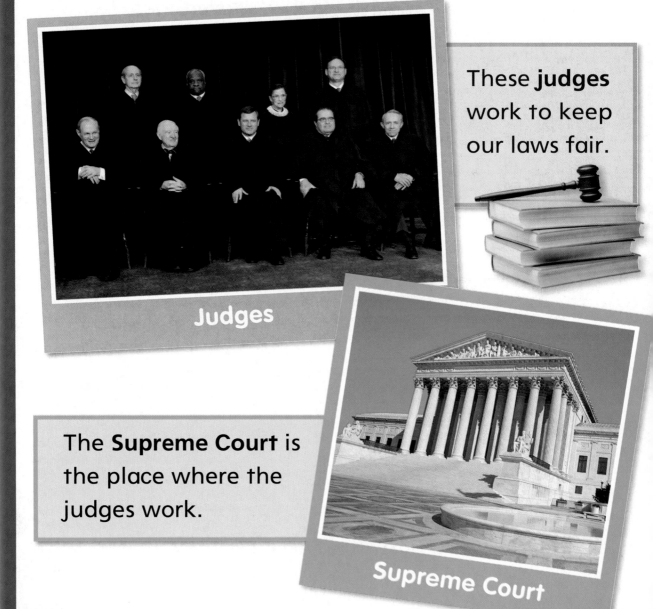

Judges

These **judges** work to keep our laws fair.

The **Supreme Court** is the place where the judges work.

Supreme Court

A Judge Is Appointed

John Roberts was **appointed** by the President to be a **judge** on the Supreme Court.

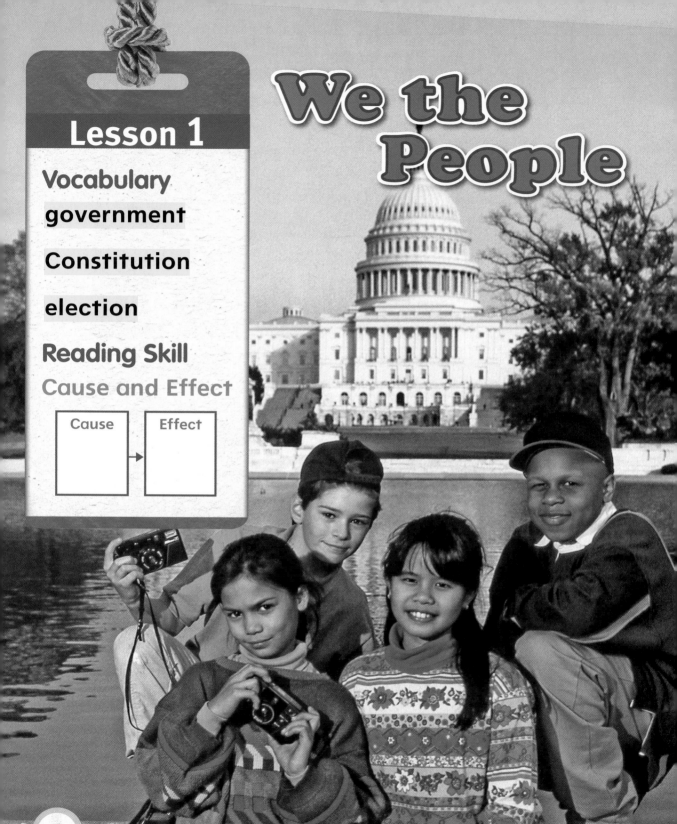

We the People

Vocabulary

government

Constitution

election

Reading Skill

Cause and Effect

Cause		Effect
	→	

Our Government

Government helps big groups of people get along. A government is all of the people who run a community, state, or country. Government workers meet to find ways to make our lives better.

 What is government?

Government workers talk about a new law.

Our first leaders plan the Constitution.

Our Constitution

Our country's first leaders worked hard to plan a good government. They wanted a fair government that would keep people safe and free.

The plan they wrote is called the **Constitution**. The Constitution says that our government is run by its citizens.

The Constitution says that we choose our own leaders. It says that each state helps to decide on our laws. It also says that we are free to say and write what we think. It says that we are free to choose our religion.

 What are three things our Constitution says?

Event
Indiana Becomes a State

Indiana became a state on December 11, 1816. It was the 19th state to become a part of the United States of America.

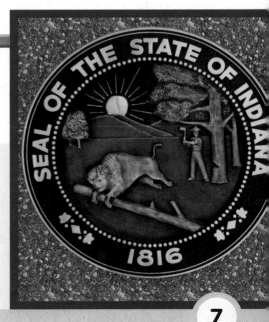

Citizens Rule

One way citizens rule our government is by voting. Citizens vote to choose our leaders and lawmakers. Citizens also vote to choose new laws. The special time when citizens vote is called an **election**.

By voting, citizens control government. So, we say that the United States government is of the people, by the people, and for the people.

 How do citizens rule our country?

Check Understanding

1. **Vocabulary** What is an **election**?

2. **Cause and Effect** How are government leaders chosen?

3. How does government help us?

Vocabulary

judge

Congress

court

Supreme Court

Reading Skill

Cause and Effect

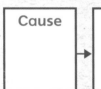

Cause	Effect

Our Country's Government

Three Parts of Government

Our government is divided into three parts. Each part is run by a different group of people. The three groups are leaders, lawmakers, and **judges**. A judge is the person who decides what our laws mean.

Our Constitution says that our leaders, lawmakers, and judges must work together. That way, one part of our government will not have too much power.

 What three groups run our government?

leaders

lawmakers

The Three Parts of Government

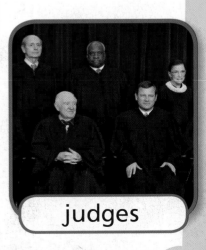

judges

Our Leaders, Our Lawmakers

The President is the leader of our country. The President's job is to make sure everyone follows the laws of our country. He works with leaders from other countries, too. We vote to choose our President once every four years.

Around the World

Great Britain is a country in Europe. It was once ruled by kings and queens. Today, the leader of Great Britain is called the prime minister.

Congress

All of our country's lawmakers together are called **Congress**. Congress makes laws for the people of our country. First, lawmakers talk and write about an idea for a new law. Then, Congress votes "yes" or "no" to decide if the idea should become a law.

 What is the President's job?

Our Judges

Judges work in a place called a **court**. The most important court in our country is the **Supreme Court**. It is in Washington, D.C. Judges in the Supreme Court make sure that our laws agree with our Constitution.

In a court, a judge decides what is fair. A judge decides if a person has broken a law. If the person has broken a law, the judge may decide on a punishment.

 What is a judge's job?

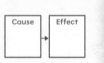

Check Understanding

1. **Vocabulary** What is a **court**?

2. **Cause and Effect** What happens after Congress talks and writes about an idea for a law?

Cause	Effect

3. Why do the three parts of our government work together?

Citizenship

Points of View

What makes a good leader?

These second graders are from Indiana. Read about what they think makes a person a good leader.

Indiana

"A good leader is fair and helps others. He or she listens to people and makes smart choices so people don't feel left out. A good leader stands up for what they believe in."

Ava Mendez Ramos

Ava Mendez Ramos

"A good leader can be in charge without being bossy. A good leader cares about your feelings and makes plans that include everyone."

Claire Madison

Claire Madison

"A good leader knows what to do when people don't agree. My family could not agree on a name for our new puppy. My uncle told us the fair way to choose a name is to vote."

Jamil Shomari

Jamil Shomari

Our Country's Capital

Vocabulary

capital

Capitol

diagram

monument

Reading Skill

Cause and Effect

Cause	Effect

Washington, D.C.

The city of Washington, D.C., belongs to all people in the United States. It is called the **capital** of the United States. A capital city is where government workers work.

Washington, D.C., has many important buildings. The **Capitol** building is where Congress makes laws for our country.

 What is a capital city?

The White House

The White House is the building where the President lives and works. The White House has many rooms.

The **diagram** on the next page shows the inside of the White House. A diagram is a picture that shows the parts of something.

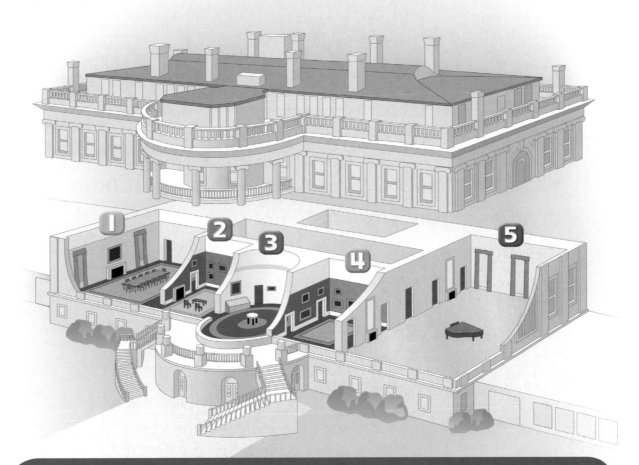

The White House

1 **State Dining Room** The President and guests eat dinner here.

2 **Red Room** First Lady Eleanor Roosevelt met news reporters here.

3 **Blue Room** President Grover Cleveland got married in this room.

4 **Green Room** President James Monroe liked to play cards here.

5 **East Room** This is the largest room in the White House. It is used for concerts, dances, and large meetings.

 Which is the largest room in the White House? How is the room used?

Monuments

There are many **monuments** in Washington, D.C. A monument is a building or statue that shows special respect for a person or event. The Washington Monument shows respect for our first President.

The Jefferson Memorial shows our respect for our third President, Thomas Jefferson. He wrote the Declaration of Independence.

Jefferson
Memorial

Washington
Monument

Abraham Lincoln was one of our greatest Presidents. A monument called the Lincoln Memorial helps us remember how he cared about freedom for all.

 Can you name three Presidents?

 Lincoln Memorial

Check Understanding

1. **Vocabulary** What is the **Capitol** building?

2. **Cause and Effect** Why do people build monuments?

Cause	Effect

3. 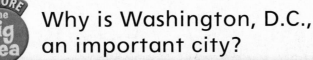 Why is Washington, D.C., an important city?

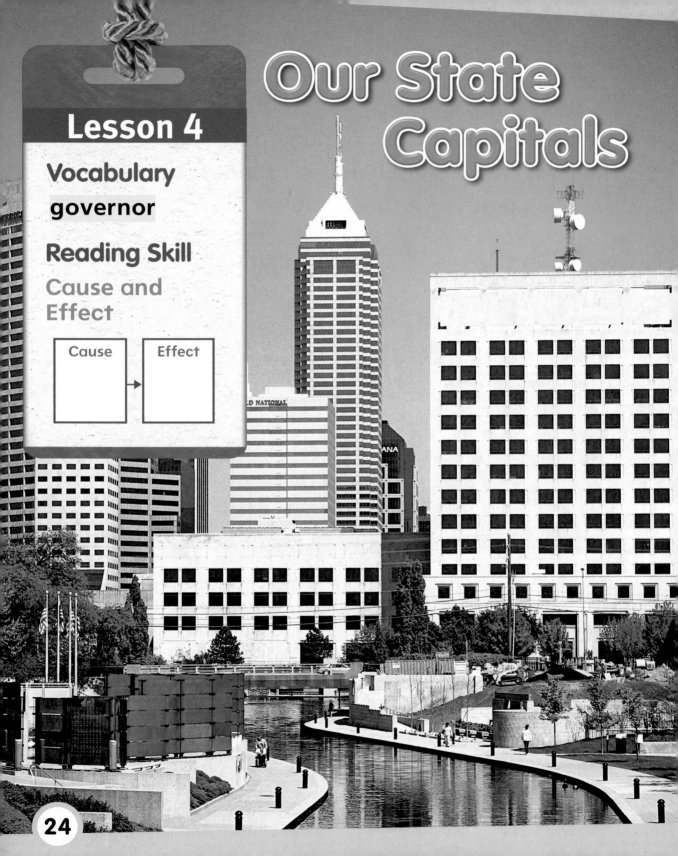

Our State Capitals

Lesson 4

Vocabulary
governor

Reading Skill

Cause and Effect

Cause		Effect
	→	

Capital Cities

Each of our 50 states has its own capital city. For example, Indianapolis is the capital city of Indiana.

Every capital city has its own capitol building. State leaders, lawmakers, and judges work in the capitol building that is located in their capital city.

 What is your state's capital city?

Indiana State Capitol building in Indianapolis

State Government

Each state has a government with three parts. Like the government of our country, each state has a leader, lawmakers, and judges.

The leader of a state is called the **governor**. Citizens of a state vote for the governor and state lawmakers.

Mitch Daniels is the governor of Indiana.

Places
Governor's Residence

The governor's residence of Indiana was built in 1928 in the capital of Indianapolis. There are 23 rooms and 11 restrooms in the residence.

The Supreme Court of Indiana has five judges.

Each state has a state supreme court. Each state also has its own constitution. The judges follow the state constitution to make sure the state laws are fair.

 How is state government like the government of our country?

State Symbols

You know that our country's flag belongs to everyone. But, did you know that each state has its own flag, too? Ohio's state flag has a blue triangle that stands for hills and valleys. The circle stands for the "O" in the word Ohio.

Our country's flower is the red rose. Our country's bird is the bald eagle. Each state has its own bird and flower, too. Wisconsin's state flower is the violet.

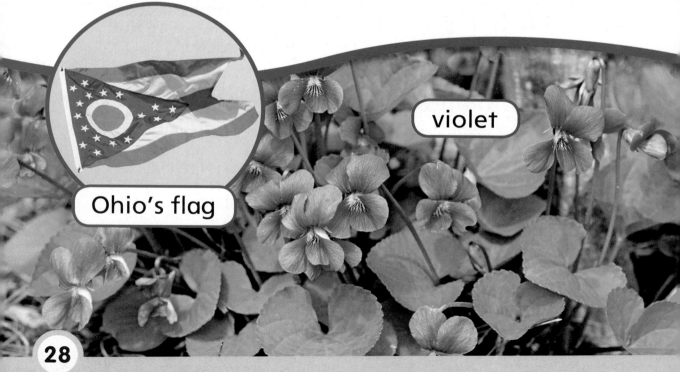

violet

Ohio's flag

The Illinois state bird is the cardinal. What is your state's flower and bird?

 What kinds of symbols does your state have?

cardinal

Check Understanding

1. **Vocabulary** What is a **governor**?

2. **Cause and Effect** How is the state governor chosen?

Cause	Effect

3. Where do state leaders, lawmakers, and judges work?

Use a Compass Rose

Vocabulary

compass rose

Look at the symbol below. It is called a **compass rose**. A compass rose has arrows that point to the letters **N**, **S**, **E**, and **W**. These arrows show the directions north, south, east, and west.

Look at the map of Indiana. Can you find the compass rose?

Places to Visit in Indiana

- Amish Country
- Indiana Beach
- Indianapolis Speedway
- Turkey Run State Park and Covered Bridges
- Holiday World and Splashin' Safari

Lake Michigan

Wabash River

Lake Schafer

White River

Ohio River

N W E S

0   20   40 miles

0   20   40 kilometers

Try the Skill

1. What is a **compass rose**?

2. Is Indianapolis Speedway north or south of Amish Country?

✏️ **Writing Activity**

Write the direction you travel to go from Lake Schafer to Lake Michigan.

Lesson 5

Vocabulary
mayor

Reading Skill
Cause and Effect

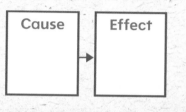

Olga Velazquez, Mayor of Portage, Indiana

Community Government

Community Leaders

Community government is also made up of three parts. Leaders, lawmakers, and judges in a city work in a building called city hall.

In many communities, the leader is called the **mayor**. A mayor makes sure that community laws are followed. Greg Ballard is the mayor of Indianapolis, Indiana.

 Who works at city hall?

Mayor Greg Ballard celebrates on election night.

The city council of Bloomington, Indiana

Lawmakers and Judges

Community lawmakers meet to make laws and solve problems for the community. In Bloomington, Indiana this group of lawmakers is called the city council.

In Bloomington, if you break a law you may have to go to a community court. For example, littering is against the law in Bloomington. A person who litters might have to go to a court and see a judge.

 What is the group of lawmakers in Bloomington called?

Check Understanding

1. **Vocabulary** What is a **mayor**?

2. **Cause and Effect** Why might a person have to see a judge?

Cause	Effect

3. 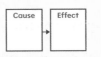 Why does the city council meet?

Vocabulary

justice

immigrant

Reading Skill

Cause and Effect

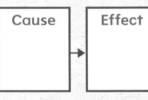

Cause		Effect
	→	

Justice for All

The Pledge of Allegiance

Our flag stands for freedom and **justice**. Justice means fairness. We make a promise to be loyal to our country when we say the Pledge of Allegiance to our flag.

Pledge of Allegiance

I pledge allegiance to the flag
of the United States of America
and to the republic for which it stands,
one Nation under God, indivisible,
with liberty and justice for all.

 What does our flag stand for?

Coming to America

America is a nation of **immigrants**. An immigrant is a person who leaves one country to live in another.

Long ago most immigrants sailed to America on ships. They could see the Statue of Liberty when they arrived at Ellis Island in New York. The Statue of Liberty stands for freedom.

Statue of Liberty

Millions of immigrants from around the world have come to live in America. Today people still come to make America their home. Some come to live in freedom. Others come to make a better life.

 What are some reasons that people come to America?

These immigrants are becoming American citizens.

Working for Justice

America has a tradition of working hard for freedom and fairness. Years ago women in our country were not allowed to vote. Elizabeth Cady Stanton and Susan B. Anthony knew that this was not fair.

Susan B. Anthony and Elizabeth Cady Stanton

Anthony talked to lawmakers in Congress. Stanton and Anthony wrote a newspaper. They led marches. They worked hard for a new law that allowed women to vote.

Today all citizens over age 18 can vote. Our country became more fair because of these women.

How did Stanton and Anthony work for justice?

The law changed in 1920. Women could vote!

Rosa Parks

Leaders for Justice

Rosa Parks was a leader for justice. One unfair law said that black people had to give up their seats to white people on buses. Parks would not give up her seat to a white person. Police took her to jail.

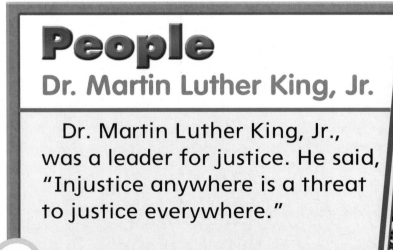

People
Dr. Martin Luther King, Jr.

Dr. Martin Luther King, Jr., was a leader for justice. He said, "Injustice anywhere is a threat to justice everywhere."

Dr. Martin Luther King, Jr., helped Rosa Parks. He told people to stop riding buses until the unfair bus law was changed. The United States government listened when Parks and King stood up for justice.

 How did Martin Luther King, Jr., help?

Check Understanding

1. **Vocabulary** What is **justice**?

2. **Cause and Effect** How did Rosa Parks help to change a law?

Cause	Effect

3. **EXPLORE The Big Idea** What things can people do to change unfair laws?

Review and Assess

Vocabulary

Number a paper from 1 to 3. Next to each number write the word that matches the meaning.

| Congress | judge | Supreme Court |

1. a person who decides if a law was broken

2. lawmakers who work in Washington, D.C.

3. the most important court in our country

Critical Thinking

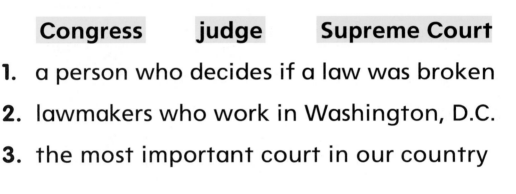

4. Do you know someone who would be a good leader? Why?

5. How is the United States government like state government?

Skill

Use a Compass Rose

Look at the compass rose and map.
Answer the question below.

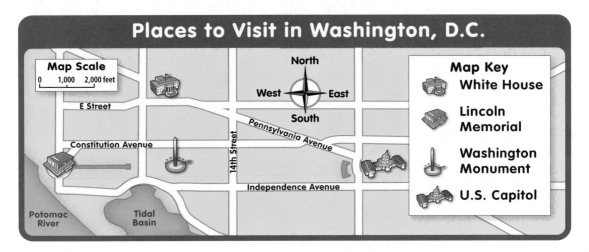

Places to Visit in Washington, D.C.

Map Scale
0   1,000   2,000 feet

E Street

Constitution Avenue

14th Street

Pennsylvania Avenue

Independence Avenue

Potomac River

Tidal Basin

North
West — East
South

Map Key
White House
Lincoln Memorial
Washington Monument
U.S. Capitol

6. In which direction do you travel to get from the U.S. Capitol to the Lincoln Memorial?

A. north

B. south

C. east

D. west

Government Activity

Make a Symbols Mobile

1 Draw and label pictures of our country's flag, bird, and flower on index cards.

2 Find out about your own state's flag, bird, and flower.

3 On the back of the three index cards, draw and label your own state's flag, bird, and flower.

4 Attach the pictures to a coat hanger.

Ruffed Grouse

Mountain Laurel

Flag

Picture Glossary

C

capital The city where the people of our government work. *Indianopolis is the capital city of Indiana.* (page 19)

Capitol The building where lawmakers work. *The Capitol building is located in Washington, D.C.* (page 19)

compass rose A symbol on a map that has arrows that point out the directions north, east, south, and west. *The compass rose helped us find our way south from the Toledo Zoo to the Ohio State Capitol.* (page 30)

Congress All of our country's lawmakers together. *We saw where Congress works when we visited Washington, D.C.* (page 13)

Constitution The plan for our government. *The Constitution says that we are free to say and write what we think.* (page 6)

court A place where judges work. *This court is located in St. Louis, Missouri.* (page 14)

D

diagram A picture with labels to tell what things are. *This **diagram** shows the different parts of the White House.* (page 20)

E

election The special time when we vote for our leaders and new laws. *We had an **election** to vote for a President.* (page 8)

G

government The group of people who lead a community, state, or country. ***Government** workers meet to find ways to make our lives better.* (page 5)

governor The leader of a state. *The citizens of Massachusetts elected Deval Patrick to be the new **governor**.* (page 26)

I

immigrant A person who leaves one country to live in another. *My great grandmother was an **immigrant** from Ireland.* (page 38)

J

judge A person who decides what the laws mean. ***Judges** make sure that laws are fair.* (page 11)

justice Fairness. *Susan B. Anthony cared about justice for all women.* (page 37)

mayor The leader of a community. *Greg Ballard is the mayor of Indianapolis, Indiana.* (page 33)

monument A building or a statue that shows special respect for a person or event. *The Washington Monument shows respect for our first President.* (page 22)

Supreme Court The most important court in our country. *The Supreme Court is located in Washington, D.C.* (page 14)

Index

This index lists many things you can find in your book. It tells the page numbers on which they are found. If you see the letter *m* before a page number, you will find a map on that page.

Credits